CW01573064

The Compound Heart

The Compound Heart

Selected Poems by Clementina Arderiu

Poems in Catalan
Translated by Julia Dale

This bilingual edition first published by
Francis Boutle Publishers
272 Alexandra Park Road
London N22 7BG
Tel 020 8889 8087
Email: info@francisboutle.co.uk
www.francisboutle.co.uk

Estate of Clementina Arderiu © 2019
Translations © Julia Dale 2019
All rights reserved.
No part of this book may be reproduced, stored
in a retrieval system, or transmitted, in any form
or by any means, electronic, mechanical photocopying
or otherwise without the prior permission of the publishers.

ISBN 978 1 9164906 6 6

Acknowledgements

The many Catalan friends and acquaintances who have helped me along the way, particularly Dr. Josep-Maria Pascual and Marisa Pascual, Zarinda and poetry-reading friends, and Inés Guy, whose comments and patient reading have been invaluable; also Maria and Alfonso for support and hospitality; the staff at Gerona University library, Xavier Pla, and Misia Sert, for their support; the wonderful Llibreria Geli in Girona for finding background material, and the remarkable second-hand bookshop 'Sweet Books' because it was there that I first came across a tiny edition of Arderiu's work.

Among English friends, CB1 Poets for enthusiastic reception of drafts tried out in open mic, Emily Dening for appreciating the poems and egging me on, Clare Redfern, Ann Nichols, Jane O'Neill and Kitty Hunter Blair for help and encouragement in various ways. Thankyou, everyone! And thanks to Clive Boutle, of course, for seeing this through with such imagination and patience.

Contents

Introduction

For many Catalan readers, Clementina Arderiu is a national treasure. After her success at the Barcelona 'Jocs de Flors' in 1912, she became the tutee and then wife and tireless companion of the poet and cultural pioneer Carles Riba, and with him suffered exile under Franco. Her work is infused with the wealth and subtleties of the Catalan language, in all its 19th-20th century renaissance brilliance, and her diction is rooted in local detail. To read, let alone translate, her poetry demands real attention – as she says in 'The Poem', the door to the outside must be closed, the work's mystery plumbed in solitude and silence. Hers are poems of grace, strength and subversiveness: however simple they may seem, they perplex and snag, and leave their reader wondering.

In general terms my approach to Arderiu's work is close to that of Maria-Mercè Marçal in her introduction to the anthology, *Contraclaror* (Barcelona, 1968 and 2008), in which she deconstructs the popular image of the poetess with the sweet name and devoted temperament, and explores some of the emotional tensions that emerge from her work when more closely read.

According to Marçal, these 'clarobscurs' – paradoxical blends of dark and light – are usually attributed only to the poet's personal life, her relationship with Riba, her child's death, the time in exile, etc. But Marçal suggests another perspective for many of the darker poems: Arderiu's position as a female writer in the early and mid 20th century. It was understandable then, she points out, 'that a singularly intelligent and creative woman should choose for herself – consciously (which is not to say 'freely') – the life of 'a woman like any other woman, like so many others'… and that this woman should invest so much of her energy and effort in constructing her own self in the image and likeness of a feminine ideal that was to confine and slow her down' – but contrarieties in the poems question this persona (Marçal, Introduction to *Contraclaror*, p.xxiii.).

One aspect of this feminine ideal may have its visual counterpart in

3

the 'Dolorosa', the Virgin Mother in black veil and robes, who suffers and laments all suffering, and whose 'passo' or processional statue can still stir hearts as it is carried aloft in Holy Week. There is power and endurance in this version of femininity; its roots in pre-Christian culture are evoked in 'Woman, Waiting'. But, as we recognise more clearly today – a recognition that is, as Marçal discerns, implicit in Arderiu's poems – there is confinement in a temple built by men. Poems such as 'A Song of Perfect Trust' or 'Song of the Completely Useless Day' – whose very titles undo expectations raised by the word 'Song' – blend their wit and exquisitely elegant form with a sense of restrained seething:

> If my heart's not been pierced by a thorn,
> there's a splinter of ice in my blood.

In Arderiu's poems, her down-to-earth, sun-loving-ordinary-woman persona is challenged by this unmanifested indignant rebel, and both contrast with the mysterious power in the image of the 'hostalera', who appears in two earlier poems, 'Hope', and 'Elegy'. The guesthouse lady, whose hostelry evokes a Dante-esque Limbo or waiting room after death, is a mere ghost of La Dolorosa, dry of tears, pallid and yearning, but still in the role of long-suffering endurance. There is another hint of the Dolorosa's role in the later poem, 'Still Hope/Wait Still', the title of which has multiple translations (see below).

These different stances are all valid, and they complement as well as contrast with one another. Arderiu's feminism is implicit, genuinely, and its peculiar strength lies in a blend, a 'compound', of acceptance and challenge. Her 'composite' heart is both with her family and/or husband, and free to take flight, she lives out in the sun ('Undying Hope') and prefers the north-facing slopes (as in 'High Hopes'). A poem about ambition celebrates solidity and contentment; another on freedom adds a question-mark to its title. A serene-sounding lyric may have a startling, even explosive image at its centre – the shattered glass in 'Resolve', for example – while a poem that explores her pioneering urge as a poet may suddenly stress her minority, her frailty even ('To Hope', and 'Night and the Sea').

Many of her poems deal directly with anxiety or fear, where the circumstantial blurs with existential – as in 'Ventada' ('Storm Force', written during the civil war), where she feels:

4

            ... a constant shadow
            haunting my eyes –

Against such powerful evocations of distress, there are moments of defiance; sorrow may do its worst but love somehow balances the scales ('L'esperança encara dansa…').

   And it is by the elusive ideal of 'Esperança', above all, that Clementina Arderiu sought to define herself. In Catalan the noun is always forward-looking in the sense of 'hope' or 'expectancy'. But to translate the verb, 'esperar,' into English is to be confronted by a contradiction, or paradox: it may be 'hope', or 'expect' in a forward-looking sense – including that of pregnancy or poem as gestation – or on the other hand, just 'wait'. In 'Still Hope (Wait Still)' – 'Espera, encara' – 'encara' can mean still, even now, or more positively. 'just a bit longer' or 'in spite of everything'. The tension between all these alternative meanings is intense. As in the much earlier 'The Slope', the poet seems to be experiencing a personal Calvary; in the former, she struggles up a remote Parnassus hostile to women – here, she evokes a desert of gnawing grief that leads nowhere –

            …where nothing blooms
            but stones.

The silent command from the gaze of implacable angels – 'espera' – rebukes her for her moment of despair and rage, but remains ambivalent; is she to wait for more strength to go on, or go on hoping in order to be strong? – What is it, to have (and show) enough virtue? Then there's the ambivalent 'encara', shifted to the start of the angels' sentence and thus reversing the word-order of the poem's title. On one hand it emphasises a cool, perhaps critical, analysis of the poet's suffering as a lack, and at the same time, coveys compassion, a recognition of her need. The very breath of hope is then uttered – 'espera' – without the constraint of 'encara'. This single word is the last line of the poem. Its translation into monosyllabic 'wait' captures the bleakness, but not the tender consolation, of 'espera'; even with the added 'hope', it's rather tight-lipped; but 'take heart', while certainly implied, is too down-to-earth.

   I have included one poem in which the dichotomous readings are such that there are two significantly different versions possible in English from the single original – this is 'Together, Travelling', where I have followed the lead from the divergent meanings of 'soldat' to provide two whole versions – their separation helps us to appreciate the amazing

5

'composite' quality of the original. In a graphic novel they could appear as speech-bubble and thought-bubble – but being poems, they do not reveal which text is text, and which sub-text. This 'compound'-ness is another aspect special to Arderiu's poetry; the title of this selection alludes to the image of the heart in stanza 2 of 'Coup de Maître':

> Swinging in water
> my compound heart, dilated,
> rocks like a boat.

Trained as a silversmith, the poet often appears absorbed in the principles of chemistry, the breath-stopping moments of change that may go well or fail, the paradox that pure gold or silver has to be alloyed to be strong enough to make a perfect ring. She knows how to solder. And while she remarked that she never really enjoyed the work, preferring to read voraciously, and to write, it keeps showing its 'mark' in her poetic craft, which is meticulous in form but flexible, especially in its syntactic play.

Silverwork and related concepts appear quite often in the imagery – the whole idea of self-transformation has a special colour to it, whether she reflects on her 'density' ('High Hopes') or inner turmoil ('Song of the Completely Useless Day'), or marvels at the alchemy of language ('Fresh Encounter') – there is an abiding sense of chemistry, of process, of tangible ferment, and her excitement and fear around childbirth has a similar energy (Oriol). Like Seamus Heaney, for Arderiu part of the joy of poetry is working with an implement in her hand; her pen is her burin. Formally, much of her best work is in small, finely finished lyrics whose terseness can be startling, whose outward delicacy can pack a powerful punch (e.g. 'My Song', or 'A Song of Perfect Trust').

Other material things that characterise her work are the crystal glass – perhaps a mirror, or simply the clear flawless stuff, the material of the bell-jar that, long before Plath, symbolises the side of her that is protected, almost cosseted, encased and limited, but still receptive to light. Its shattering alluded to in the poem called 'Fermança' is unexplained, and regrets for this given short shrift by the busy, onward-rushing stream that the poet is questioning. Material things anchor, reassure, but are at risk of being lost, especially in war or exile; they create a vivid environment in these poems, then vanish: curtains, ladles, soft gauze, keys, cushions, account-books, door hinges that creak, draughty windows, oil in a jar.

I should mention Arderiu's having read some of the writings of Rabindranath Tagore, a little of whose work I have also translated. I was amazed to come across her 1920 versions, which she calls 'interpretations', of some chapters in Tagore's 'Crescent Moon' (1913, in English revised by Yeats – was this the edition she read?). I had already noticed some 'Tagorean' elements in her poetry that may or may not have been conscious influences. For example, her particular use of the way/journey motif, and how she blends the intensely 'everyday' and local with a sense of the out-of-reach or eternal (I have also been reminded of Emily Dickinson when reading Arderiu). By 1920 Tagore had already been translated into Spanish by J. R. Jiménez and Zenobia de Camprobí; Zenobia, by 1918, had insisted on claiming that they were the 'authorised' translators, and her rendering of 'Crescent Moon' (short monologues in the voice of a child addressing his mother) is very close to the English. No wonder Arderiu, responding to the same work, carefully calls her versions 'interpretations', allowing herself some leeway for her own voice to make the Indian boy-child come to life in Catalan – to start with, setting the prose in verse. In 'Paper Boats', she characteristically reworks the material, losing none of its charm and infusing a vigour that may well have been lost in the English. Her metre and rhyme suggest a lullaby; the need to rhyme produces the occasional extra detail – e.g. the word 'franques' in the fifth stanza means 'free', which is not explicit in Tagore's 'I launch my paper boats', but is in perfect accord with the mood. More tellingly, the interaction of clouds and boats is no longer so competitive in the Arderiu version; instead of a 'race' between them we have an 'avinença', an agreement, deal or concord. And in stanza four, the first two lines in Catalan are truly 'Tagorean', echoing imagery from earlier chapters of 'Crescent Moon' and many of his songs:

the still unopened buds of dawn
with calyces still wet…

Yet in 'Paper Boats' itself Tagore simply mentions 'shiuli' (a jasmine that flowers in autumn and drops its petals overnight), with none of the detail of petals and dew that Arderiu supplies. These poem-boats are as much hers as his, and perhaps more in tune with the original Bengali.

I have also included one poem with a specifically religious theme – 'Al Bon Papa Joan XIII'. There are many reasons why Saint John XIII is singled out as a 'Good' pope; Arderiu emphasises the reforms he made, simplifying liturgy and allowing it in different languages, and setting the foundations for the second Vatican council before he died in 1962/3. The poem comes at the end of part I of Arderiu's last published volume: 'L'esperança, encara' (the comma, emphatic, also separates it from a previously published poem in 'És a dir'). The book gathers and arranges both new and as-yet unpublished work into three parts, 'Pelegrina vinc' ('Here as a Pilgrim'), 'La taula del Rey' ('The King's Table'), and 'Després' ('Afterwards'). Many have an occasional feel, often with a devotional theme, and are often dedicated to friends or family. They are clearly not really 'public' in intention, but are a reminder of how religion was, for Arderiu, part of daily life – there's no self-consciousness about poems to the Virgin Mary or celebrating a first communion. They are composed with warmth and a lightness of touch; in this poem, she admires a pope whose love of God *and people* was a relief from the fascist-leaning pomposities of the church under Franco. Her last volume also contains poems of masterful intensity, showing that Arderiu could still write profoundly in lyrical form – the last two in my selection also end Marçal's 'Contraclaror'.

A translation is never entirely 'finished', even less so than a poem; but this selection comprises my best endeavour to give a convincing voice in English to Arderiu. I avoid mechanical imitation of verse but, especially in the earlier more formal pieces, try to capture as much as possible of the rhythm and tone. Clementina's insistence on using 'everyday' language is something I've sought to honour without straying too far into my own idiom – I don't think she would want to be 'kept in aspic'. Even her early work shows a variety of style, from the classical elegance of 'Retorn' to the strikingly modern ('El pendís') and lyrics that echo traditional folksong. She can also be 'hermetic'. In a letter to Paulina Crusat in June 1953, Carles Riba alludes to an element of the 'inaccessible' in his wife's poetry, and there are wonderfully 'impossible' moments (to translate 'dring' with any single word is as clumsy as rendering Basho's sublime 'mizuno-oto' in his frog haiku as 'plop')! At other times the terse, vivid images seem to slide quite willingly into their English equivalents. All in all, within the limits of translation, this selection aims to give English readers 'access'. J.Corredor Matheos informs us, in the prologue to his anthology (Madrid 1962, Castilian and Catalan parallel texts), that the poems of Arderiu have been translated into various languages including English, but of the last I have found no trace so far, and believe that a modern English translation of this visionary voice is long overdue.

The
Compound
Heart

A L'ESPERANÇA

Oh Esperança matinera
i joconda a l'esperit!
Tu que fas la dolor enrera
i et decantes al sentit,
repetint el mot ja dit
enllaçat al mot «Espera»;
tu que esguardes fit a fit
i esvaeixes el neguit
de la llarga carretera,
i ens allunyes el convit
de la pàlida hostalera
que propícia allà ens espera
en el terme migpartit
d'ara és dia – ara és nit;
tu que tens la caballera
de maragdes, i el vestit,
i de verd has colorit
l'herba del meu prat lleugera,
fes-me eterna dins el pit
l'alta estrofa volandera,
amb la deixa de neguit
de cercar el mot no dit.
Si tu em fossis mainadera!
D'ençà que Amor m'ha colpit,
caminar sola m'esvera:
sóc l'infant emperesit
que resta sempre endarrera,
fins que tu l'has acollit
a l'escalf suau del pit.

Oh Esperança! si és escrit,
vine – o vés-t'en ben lleugera.

To Hope

You're up at crack of dawn –
up to cheer my spirit! You
leave all misery behind,
as you pour yourself into
a word's meaning, make it new,
repeating so that it's tied in
with *wait, hope*. You face down
my restless doubts (*the way so long…*) –
they vanish at one look from you.
You steer us away, if we are drawn
to that pale hostess of the inn
who beckons at the boundary-stone
in twilight, when you can't say *now
it's day*, or *now, the night has come*.
You've emerald in your hair, your gown,
and with one gentle dab of green
you've brightened all my meadow –
deep in my heart, renew
the eternal, unbound,
the flight of poetry! Urge me on,
unfaltering in my quest, to woo
and win the word as yet unspoken –
be my Nurse – my go-between!
Since Love let fly at me, I've been
too timid to journey on my own;
I'm like a dawdling toddler, who
stubbornly hangs back, till you
scoop me up to your bosom
and hold me, safe and warm.

Oh, Hope, if it is written, come;
or, lightly, slip away.

RETORN

Com un que, fatigat i tot mesquí
després del feinejar de tot un dia,
se'n torna al seu casull, i res voldria
llevat d'un mos de pa i un bla dormir,
així jo feia via en mon camí.
I com ell só arribada i reposava
i deixava la son en mon coixí
i el mos prenia i me n'acontentava,
i l'endemà era festa: vet aquí.

Ara, però, és tot això debades:
la festa ja és passada, i el fatic.
Quan l'home aquell avui torna a les prades
mostra a sos ulls la gleva un verd més ric;
que al vespre començava d'enyorar-se,
com qui fa dies que no veu l'amic.
i a mi suara em retornava esparsa
la recordança del fatic antic.

I el dolç repos i les callades hores
també ja em començaven a pesar.
Claror i desig vull a les meves vores,
i una eina de treball dintre la mà;
que l'esperit vigili ben alerta
i aturi l'importú que ve a trucar,
que si el Tedi trobava porta oberta,
mai més l'Amor seuria en mon llindar.

RETURNING

As one who, weary and outworn
after toiling the whole day through,
comes back to his dwelling, and wants no more
than a morsel of bread and a soft bed –
so wearily I hastened on my journey.
Like him, I would arrive, ready to rest,
surrender into sleep upon my cushion –
would have my morsel, be content with it –
No work tomorrow, ah – and so lie down.

But where's the use in resting now?
The holiday's gone, and tiredness with it.
Now, when that same man goes out to the meadow,
the land looks greener, richer, to his eyes –
when evening comes, he starts to yearn for it
as if for a friend he's missed for days and days.
So, as I toiled, too, the memories were few
and fleeting, of the old weariness.

And sweet repose, or a silent hour,
for me, in turn, began to pall.
I now want light and longing on my path,
and in my hand, a tool that I can work with,
and spirit, ever wide awake, to bar
the way to any nuisance that comes knocking –
lest old Dullness find the door ajar,
and Love for ever vanish from my threshold.

Cançó de la bella confiança

A l'amat he donades
totes les claus;
jo tinc totes les seves,
i fem les paus.

Però resta una cambra
al fons del fons
on entrar no podríem
ni breus segons.

Tantes forces ocultes,
tantes pensaments
allà dins són escàpols
a tots moments!

Bé seria debades
sotjar-hi un poc:
l'aldarull colperia
més que no un roc.

Contentem-nos d'una ombra
o d'un ressò.
Que ell es dugui els seus comptes
com me'ls duc jo.

A SONG OF PERFECT TRUST

My true-love has
all my keys.
I have all his.
Peace reigns.

But there's still
the cellar,
where either would be ill-
advised to enter;

where dark forces, black
thoughts lurk –
waiting in the murk
to be unlocked.

No point in chancing
even a peek:
something rock-hard might hurtle
out of the chaos…

Enough, then, just a hint –
a shadow, a faint echo.
Let him keep his accounts.
I'll mind mine, too.

El pendís

Jo deia ahir:
ésser i sentir,
fortuna rara.
Per qué la gent – rosec mesquí –
no se n'amara,
d'ésser i sentir?
I era per mi
goig pur. Mes ara,

per un pendís
rodoladís
jo faig ma via.
Un pas amunt i en llisco sis.
Si defallia,
per mon pendís
tan dret i llis
rodolaria.

Si em vull salvar,
bé cal pujar,
no mirar enrere.
Enlaire sols puc esguardar,
que en la vorera
l'herba es secà
i es revoltà
sa cabellera.

I els arbres són
d'un son pregon
la immòbil presa;
tot el brancatge acota el front,
i gran feresa
dins mi es difon.
Sóc no sé on,
res no es palesa.

THE SLOPE

Yesterday, I'd say:
To be, to feel,
what luck!
Why gnaw at it, or pinch and scrape,
why not live steeped
in being, feeling? –
It was, to me,
sheer joy. But

this cliff's now
my path –
precipitate:
one step up and a slither
six steps down.
To falter
would be to helter-
skelter, somersault.

If I'm to survive
I must ascend –
not look behind.
I must keep looking up, strive
towards a verge
where stiff sedge,
parched, stands
hair on end,

and trees, transfixed,
succumb to sleep's
unfathomed deep –
each branch a sunken head.
Wilderness spreads
within me, rampant,
I darken, lost –
wholly perplexed.

Res ni ningú
no se m'enduu.
La mà amorosa,
l'esguard serè i el pas segur,
la remorosa
parla d'algú
que al cor tan nu
fos venturosa,

tot, lentament,
sense frisament,
fuig de ma ruta.
Pel món tingués com el morent
l'ànima eixuta,
i aquell frement
deseiximent
que res no immuta!

Nothing, no one
to free me. No gentle
touch of a hand,
soothing gaze, sure footfall.
No murmured words
that might, to a soul
so naked, sound
a welcoming note.

One after another,
slowly, all
desert my path.
Now like the dying let me feel
the world has withered –
and that shudder
of abandon:
irreversible.

ELEGIA

Oh Mort que ets tan amatent
que mai no et jugi la presa!
Darrera de ta escomesa,
a cada porta un lament.

I a cada lleu moviment,
aquella por de topar-te,
que el teu record no s'aparta
i ens torba sempre la ment.

Tant ens voltaves devant
– ahir finava l'amiga,
avui la servanta antiga,
demà, quins altres seran? –
que alhora amb els qui s'en van
un poc de nosaltres fina;
fas com l'artera veïna:
cada dia un pas avant.

I al llarg d'aquest lent finar
debades l'ànima espera,
com pensarosa hostalera
que mai no veu arribar
qui magnifique el seu pa;
i en tant els hostes s'en vénen
i passen i no s'entenen
i memòria no en restà.

Però tu hi tornes sovint,
oh freda, a la nostra estada,
i ens la fas tota poblada
de morts, sense dir-nos quin
hauràs triat en venint
quan novament ens arribes;
ara ens els portes a estibes,
més de deu i més de vint.

ELEGY

So swift, O Death, so eager –
no sleight can dodge your prey.
You swoop, and leave a dirge
at every doorway.

And, with each slight stir,
that dread of meeting you –
those memories that refuse
to fade, brewing nightmares.

You circle over us
so often – yesterday
my friend, and now our long-loved servant,
tomorrow… who's to say?
Now, part of ourselves
dies, with each departure:
day by day, like a sly neighbour,
you're one step closer.

After this slow denouement,
the soul forlornly waits –
like the sad hostess of a lodging-house
hoping someone will spare a word
of praise for her fine bread –
and all the while, guests come and go
indifferently, without trace,
not one remembered.

But you keep coming back here – you,
cold creature, to haunt our sojourn,
filling it with a whole population
of dead souls, not disclosing who
you've singled out – what loser's
been picked, this time round.
These days, you bring in plenty –
stack them in heaps – ten… twenty…

I aquests són inconeguts
– que els prens en llunyanes terres,
entre les brunes desferres,
damunt dels conreus perduts –
Oh els cossos que et són venuts
per les obscures renyines!
Oh mans folles i mesquines
que te'ls donen ja retuts!

I als ulls del nostre esperit
van passant tots cada dia,
i una nova cortesia
– gest de tan pregon sentit
que ens deixa l'esguard humit –
et fem ara tots alhora,
perquè anunciïs l'hora
de la nostra última nit.

And they are all unknown.
You gather them from afar
in parched wastelands, where
they lie on fields left to abandon.
And, oh, the bodies you've made your own
through some blind argument –
foolish and vile, those hands
that pass them to you, ready-bound!

Passing before the mind's eye
daily they all keep
passing. Now, Death, we mind
our manners – bow, so deep
and low to you, tears blur our sight.
Together, we implore you
for news of our own hour
to come – our closing night .

BARQUES DE PAPER

Interpretacions de Rabindranath Tagore, ii

Riu avall, com cada dia,
van mis barques de paper.
Una, dues… més n'hi hauria
si més n'abastava a fer.

I els poso totes per marca
amb grosses lletres el nom,
el meu nom a cada barca,
perquè el sàpiga tothom.

Elles van ben atapides
mes barquetes al matí,
amb les flors que jo he collides
de bona hora al meu jardí.

Són les poncelles de l'alba
amb el calze encara humit,
arribant a terra salva
quan ja tombarà la nit.

Llanço al riu les barques franques,
i en alçar-me i esguardar,
veig com unes veles blanques
els tènues núvols passar.

Ja no sé quin germà els llança
del cel, aire avall, d'un vol;
perquè en tan bella avinença
llisquin amb el meu estol.

De nit, que el cap s'arrecara
dins els braços, somniant,
veig passar en llarga filera
mos vaixells vogant, vogant…

PAPER BOATS

Interpretations of Rabindranath Tagore, ii

Down the river, day by day,
my paper boats go sailing.
One, two… and more there'd be
if I had time to make them.

In capitals, each one I mark
with a name, which is my own –
my own name, on every barque,
for everyone to know.

My boats, with cargo tightly packed,
venture into the morning,
laden with flowers that I have picked
at first light, in my garden –

the still-unopened buds of dawn
with calyces still wet –
afloat till they come safe to shore
as evening turns to night.

I launch them, let them sail away,
then stand, to keep an eye,
and then I see how, like white sails,
the fine-spun clouds drift by.

What unknown brother's poured them
from heaven, down in a breeze,
to glide along in such accord,
matching my fleet with ease?

At night, when snug and warm I rest
my head in my arms, and sleep,
in a long line I see them pass –
my boats, breasting the deep…

Sota la nit estellada
voguen lluny, més lluny i més…
Nauxer que els mena, una fada,
l'estiba, somnis lleugers.

Under the starlit skies of night,
on and on, they stream…
the boatman steering them, a sprite,
their cargo, gentle dreams.

CANÇÓ DEL DIA INÚTIL

Aquest dia que fina, que fina
lentament, com la llàntia en el vas,
ne em portà l'alegria divina,
ni de mi no féu mica de cas.

Em deixà dins la cambra pregona
com un fòtil inútil i vell,
entre els mobles que fan la rodona
i les mosques que em busquen la pell.

No tingué ni la minsa sorpresa
d'una pluja o d'un vent displicent,
no mogué la cortina malmesa
ni en el sol no posà entelament.

Fou només com la fonda llossada
a les coses que em bullen a dins
i un cruixir de vianda cremada
i una olor de ferments i de vins.

Com el dia que fina, que fina,
no en voldria cap més a mon pas;
si en mon cor no posà cap espina,
féu ma sang una mica de glaç.

Song of the Completely Useless Day

Tapering slowly towards its end
the way a jug of oil runs dry,
this day has brought no celestial joy;
indifferent, it's passed me by .

Dumped in the depths of my room
like an old bit of jumble, just fit for the bin,
with tables and chairs circling round in the gloom
and mosquitoes in search of my skin,

I've been sprung no surprises – not even a jolt –
a shower, say, or a crotchety wind;
nothing to ruffle the dingy curtain,
or draw a veil over the sun.

It's been no more than a scoop – a ladle –
of all that's been boiling inside me,
the burnt stuff, its crunch and crackle,
an odour of wine, of ferment.

Like the day tapering to its end,
I feel no desire to go on;
if my heart's not been pierced by a thorn,
there's a splinter of ice in my blood.

EL MEU CANT

De no cantar
jo m'entristia:
per mi és el cant
tal como el pa
de cada dia.

És un parany,
una ferida.
Cada cançó
s'emporta un tany
de ma florida.

Però què hi fa,
quin mal hi hauria?
Jo, del meu cant,
en vull ornar
tota ma via.

My Song

Not singing made me
sad.
For me, song
is just like food –
my daily bread.

It's a fool's game,
it wounds –
each song
snaps off
a sprig in bloom.

So where's the harm?
With my song
I'll have my road
festooned –
all the way along!

TARDOR

Ja no sóc, ja no tinc,
ja no vull ni voldria.
Què no sóc? Què no tinc?
Què no vull ni voldria?
Una cosa que el temps
inclement em prenia.
Si no sóc i no tinc
tal com era i tenia,
per orgull no ho deman
ni ho prendria.

I també perquè m'és
l'hora escàpol tan blana
sota el vidre polit
de la meva campana!
Dues ratlles de sol
la presó em tornen vana.
I també perquè en mi
altra cosa ara mana,
que és més íntima i és
soberana.

LATE SEASON

No longer have, no longer am,
no longer want or would –
what am I, or have, no longer?
What no longer want, or would?
Simply what inclement time
has been stealing from me.
If I no longer am, or have,
whatever once I was, or had,
I will not stoop to plead –
or take it back, if given.

And besides, a fleeting moment
feels so soft, inside
my bell-jar's polished glass!
And with but a scratch or two
of scribbled sun, prison's rendered
void, useless. And, besides,
there is something else
that governs now,
something deep inside
that's sovereign.

RETROBAMANT

Dónes encara al meu sentit,
paraula,
l'estremiment ple de finors
d'abans;
i tens dolçors per l'ànima
infinites,
paraula, acord perfecte, so
dels anys.

Música poses bellament
difusa
damunt la meva lassitud.
I cau
fonda en el pou del mal humor
la nosa.
Or i cristall és el teu dring
– astral.

FRESH ENCOUNTER

Words, in me you still awaken
that cold
delicate shudder – that *frisson* –
as of old;
Infinitely soothing, you
delight my soul,
words, pure harmony – echo
of years gone by.

Your ethereal music
flows freely
over my lethargy.
And down tumble
my barriers, into the well
of melancholy.
You ring, like gold, like crystal –
astral.

INDICIS

Indicis. De què? Es refusen
les meves ales a fer enrere el vol:
els buits de l'espai acusen
més sòlids músculs si el camí es resol.
L'angoixa llencem, i sigui
el llast innoble que m'atura. Fi,
vingui un airet que'm digui:
«La branca encara és verda com ahir».

Signs

Signs. Of… what? My wings will not
fly backwards: Once on course,
against the voids of space they set
their firmness of muscle.
Let's jettison worry, cut free
of all unworthy ballast.
Just bring me a breath of air that says to me:
The branch is still as green as yesterday.

AL BOSC DE MEVA SON

Al bosc de la meva son
anàvem. De mi no resta,
en ser-hi, sinó el record.
Caçades al llaç, vergonya!
mes falles totes hi són.
Jo em veia com la regina
inútil sense la cort.
M'ajeia contra la terra,
batuda i sense perdó;
els ulls miraven miraven
tanta fullaraca d'or:
els ulls miraven i veien
ran de terra viure un món.
El pigot, per si calia,
m'esvera amb el seu renou
i amb el seu vol se m'enduia
del bosc de la meva son.

DREAM-WOOD

Into the woods I dreamed
we made our way.
Then all I remember is…
Trapped in the hunter's snare
– the shame of it! –
all my faults, my failures.
I see myself – an impotent queen
who's lost her court. I'm on the ground.
Thrashed. But not absolved.
I stare up at dead leaves –
what wastes of gold!
Wide-eyed, I gaze
down at the earth, and see
a whole world come to life…
The sudden drilling of a woodpecker
jolts me – it flies off – and I
am lifted up, away from my Dream-Wood.

ALEGRIA

Cos meu, solellada
turbulència roja:
plenitud que salta
desbridada i folla.
Alegria! Bandera
coronant la torre –
bastides no calen
ni cordes ni noses…

Roda, roda, roda,
animeta meva,
no secreta, fonda…
Cerca, mira, parla,
cenyeix graciosa,
domina i acaba
amb ta pura força
la meva ventura…

Intactes, les hores
em facin corona.

REJOICING

Body of mine, sun-
drenched tumult of red:
mad with abundance
surging, unbridled –
Joy! bright flag, fluttering
high up on the turret –
no need for scaffolding,
no ropes to hold it down…

Free-wheeling, all around
set out, young soul of mine –
not hidden, but profound –
seek, gaze, parley.
Firm, ever-unspoiled,
let graceful wit, your girdle,
steady me in its circle
whatever may unfold…

Unadulterated
hours, weave me my crown!

CONTINUÏTAT

De mi no sé, ni mai saber podría
   – voluble línia –
com per la meva voluntat probable
   seré menada;
ni si la pròdiga esperança viva
   – com jo d'antiga –
capbusserà dins una mar revolta
   – dofins i aurores.

Només és cert que a la final clausura,
   quan tot acusa,
veure podré com una corda tensa
   ma vida feta.

CONTINUITY

I cannot tell, nor ever could
   – the line keeps circling –
how my own will, in future, may
    direct me.
Nor whether wastrel hope, so full of life
    as, long ago, I was,
will plunge into a riotous sea –
    dolphins and new dawns.

I'm only sure that when the final close-down
    points its finger,
I shall see – like a string, drawn tight –
    my life, complete.

AMBICIÓ

Sobre el nus perfecte
de la juventud,
aturada serva't,
vida meva. Pugui
de la suma exacta
del cabal hagut
no llevar-ne encara
unitat ni zero.
Que la força densa
que domina en mi
posi a cada anyada
la mateixa inèrcia.
I passin les tardes
en un bell seguir,
com doll que refresca
el quintà i l'obaga.

High Hopes

Here on the very
nub of youth,
stay put,
life of mine.
I would not subtract
a single jot
from just this amount
of flow.
Let the sheer force
of my solidity
reap, each harvest,
the same inertia.
And may my afternoons slip by
in sweet pursuit, like a spring
refreshing the home terrain
the shady, north-facing slopes.

CAMINEM ACOSTATS

Caminem acostats
com soldats;
i he parlat de companyia
quan més sola que mai em sentia.

La ventura, ¿qui la deixa
aleshores que ella ment
tan meravellosament?

No torneu a fer-me queixa:
fugiré de mi mateixa
a tot risc i contra vent.

Caminem acostats
com soldats;
i he parlat de companyia
quan més i més que mai la defugia.

A NOTE ON THE TRANSLATION OF 'CAMINEM ACOSTATS'

The key word in this poem is 'soldats'. In the context of moving forward or journeying together, it immediately suggests 'like soldiers' – but can equally mean 'as if soldered', an image derived from the silver-work that Arderiu was trained in during her youth (see Introduction). The potential soldier's voice, which colours his sense of words like 'company', gives the poem its robustness. This emerges in 'Marching Together'.

'Soldered', however, may more closely reflect autobiographical reality – the (often reluctant) journeys the poet made while accompanying her husband on academic or literary sojourns. 'Together, Travelling' brings out this more domestic voice, for example in the translation of 'la ventura' as good fortune, the happy life, rather than the unknown to come. Both are essential to the alloy of the original; so both English versions, each needing the other, are printed overleaf.

TOGETHER, TRAVELLING

Togetherness, as we travelled,
was like being soldered –
I've talked of our 'companionship', but then,
really, I'd never felt so alone.

A happy life! – who'd turn that down
so long as it can lie so
wonderfully? – But no,

it's no use grumbling on,
I'll leave behind the self I've always known –
no matter the risk, or how the wind may blow.

We travelled as if soldered
together, and I've called it
'companionship', when, to be honest,
that was, increasingly, the last thing I wanted.

MARCHING TOGETHER

Like soldiers, we
marched in close formation –
and though I've spoken of our 'company'
I'd never felt, till then, such isolation.

The great unknown – who'd miss
the chance, while it can fool our eyes
with such exquisite lies?

No wingeing, it's no use:
forget the old self – I'm cutting loose
in the teeth of the wind, whatever the risk.

We marched in step like soldiers,
shoulder to shoulder –
in 'company', I've said. But more and more
I wanted out. More than ever before.

UNA DONA ESPERA

Món que va girant. Rellotge.
L'espera
és de sempre i només femenina?
La clara certesa immediata
no compta?

Dolor no hi val, ni metgia.
La roda
no segueix lentament implacable?
Un clima per cada alegria.
Per cada dolor, quina força
mancada!

Dessota un cel transitori
que pesa,
o en el ras solellat que fulgura,
serem – és més fort que nosaltres –
l'eterna vestal que suplica
i espera.

WOMAN, WAITING

The watchdial world keeps turning.
  Just wait…
Be patient! – is that feminine? Just that?
Does being clear, being certain – *now* –
  not count?

Aloof from suffering or cure,
  does not
the wheel turn slowly on, relentless?
A change of weather with each joy –
  with every sorrow, what
  ebbed strength!

Under a shifting, lowering sky
  that's laden,
or in a flash of sunlight over the plain,
we live out our eternal destiny:
  tending the Vestal flame
  we pray – we wait.

DE LA POR

Lànima petita
s'em fa a poc a poc.
Tinc la casa oberta,
mestressa no sóc;
feinejo debades
i amb un ai al cor:
les portes no clouen,
Déu meu, quina por!
L'ànima, petita
s'em fa a poc a poc.

Trompetes de festa,
violins d'estiu,
sonaven encara
avui com ahir –
si no desafinen
se n'hi va ben prim.
I les flors a taula
canten de desig;
dels meus fills el riure
és salt de dofins.

Però ai!, voldria
de ma por repòs.
L'esparver que temo
ja ha aixecat el vol.
La terra verdosa
se'm tara de groc.
És injust que ens lligui
la por de la mort.
I jo, ai!, voldria
de ma por repòs.

FEAR

Slowly, my soul
is shrinking.
My house, no longer mine,
lies wide open;
my chores are empty motions,
my heart is full of dread:
none of the doors will close,
and the fear – dear God!
Slowly, my soul goes on
shrinking.

Holiday fanfares,
summer violins,
play on, the same today
as yesterday –
as ever, only just
in tune…
And on the table, flowers
keep singing of love –
I hear my children laugh:
a dolphin-leap.

But oh, how much I long
for some respite from fear!
The hawk I dread
is on the wing already.
My green meadow
is spoiled with tares.
Unfair, that we should be
so shackled to Death's terror!
And I – oh, how I long
for respite from this fear!

LA GRAN JUGADA

Silenci de mirades.
Qui perd en la jugada?
Ai, dubte que t'obstines!
   Respira fort!

Per l'aigua va gronxant-se
– tumbaga dilatada –
el cor com una barca.
   Respira fort!

Que em portin verdes glasses!
La primavera passa,
la Mort vol disfrassar-se.
   Respira fort!

A dintre de la casa,
refèim la jugada;
la porta oberta frisa.
   Respira fort!

COUP DE MAÎTRE

A hush of glances.
Who's losing in this game?
Ah doubt, how you persist!
  Deep breath…

Swinging in water
my compound heart, dilated,
rocks like a boat.
  Deep breath…

Bring dressings of green gauze! –
Spring cannot last,
Death needs its disguise.
  Deep breath…

Inside, we start again.
The door's ajar.
  It creaks.
  Deep breath…

DE LA LLIBERTAT?

Començaré per dir «corria»
i ja la veig corrent:
sòc jo mateixa quan esclata
la força adolescent.
Sentia esquerpa tota cosa,
tot m'era nosa. Fi,
como un tallant, fendia l'aire
mon cos; i per fugir,
només la punta vigorosa
del peu a l'empedrat
i el braç que ritma i l'alegria
del cap escaballat.

D'aquesta empenta apassionada
prou bé tenim record.
De llibertat és una estampa
gravada al fons del cor.

FREEDOM?

I'll start with the word, 'running'
and straight off, I can see her,
legging it – it's me,
in my explosive teens.
Everything threatened to tie me down:
– it was all in the *way*! –
till my whole body felt like a blade
slicing through air – escape
could be as simple as stepping out
brisk and firm on a cobbled street,
and the rhythmic swing of an arm, and sheer
joy of loosened hair…

Let us keep good note
of this passionate momentum.
It is the stamp of freedom,
deep down, in the heart.

Ventada

Però encara no és passada,
oh cor meu!
Ha vingut escabellada,
tota urc.

Per la força – ai com crida! –
se m'enduu;
sense alè, atemorida
menjo pols.

L'amistat arremolina
– bo i dolent;
res d'amiga ni veïna
ni cel blau.

Només l'ombra que no em deixa
dintre els ulls;
em debato amb mi mateixa
i em faig mal.

La ventada té cobertes
multituds:
com un camp li són ofertes,
– tristes flors!

I esgarrifa la dallada
que va fent
amb la Mort aparellada:
quanta sang!

STORM FORCE

– But it's still not gone,
for the love of God!
It's here, swaggering around
shock-haired, respecting no one.

Brute force. Roaring.
I'm swept away –
breathless, petrified,
gulping dust.

Fellowship swirls, scatters,
good tossed with bad.
No sign of soul-mate or neighbour,
no blue sky.

Only a constant shadow
haunting my eyes –
I battle with myself.
I self-harm.

Under the wind's thumb
thousands cower
as if on some sacrificial field –
poor flowers!

And how grim, that scythe,
mowing, side by side
with Death…
so much blood!

DESASSOSSEC

Em donen aigua tèrbola
– jo veig el vi daurat.

No sento la campana
– al cor em va sonant,

Per l'aire, quina angoixa!
– els arbres són fruitats.

Quin rendiment tan pobre!
– més rica sóc que mai.

Si cal que jo naufragui,
em llançaria al mar.

DISQUIET

The water here is cloudy
   – I see sweet, golden wine.

The bell – I cannot hear it
   – deep in the heart, it chimes.

The air resounds with torment!
   – fruit-trees will soon be ripe.

The harvest, so depleted!
   – I'm richer now than ever.

If shipwreck is my lot,
let me launch out to sea.

Prec en la guerra

Perdó
de les victòries,
de les desfetes,
de les batalles
perdó,
Senyor!

No m'esgarrifa
la Mort a penes:
viure m'espanta.
Perdó,
Senyor!

El món que féreu
no us acontenta,
i ara el voldríeu
millor,
Senyor?

Gràcia pels joves
que amb ira esperen.
Per ells voldríem
blavor,
Senyor!

L'estiu s'acaba.
Raïm de serva
volíem ésser:
perdó,
Senyor!

Carroll sens nombre
que va esgranant-se
esdeveníem.
Senyor,
perdó!

WARTIME PRAYER

Forgive
the victories,
forgive the routs,
forgive us our battles –
forgive,
O Lord!

I'm barely disturbed
by Death any more –
what's fearful is life.
Forgive me,
Lord!

This world You made,
is it not good enough,
and now would You have it
better,
Lord?

Grace to the young
keeping furious watch
grant them more light
in their sky,
Lord!

Summer is over.
We wanted to be
grapes for Your harvest –
forgive us,
Lord!

In un-numbered clusters
we hang on the vine,
dropping and wasting –
O Lord,
forgive!

Desperta dintre la nit

Desperta dintre la nit,
mirava. No fos l'angoixa
– el buc de la cambra és viu,
la fosca em toca la cara,
sento el corc com mina el llit,
percebo sentors de cala
i m'acompanya un respir –
no fos l'angoixa que em serra,
bé em podria expandir.
Però veig en l'ombra negra
com em fallava el desig;
mea culpa que voldria
ostentar damunt el pit.
Ja no em diran dona forta
– jo mateix no m'ho dic
ni sé per quin mar navega
el meu provident destí:
vig unos passos que s'allunyen
– baladres i tamarius –
i unes mans que diuen, «Vine,
no t'espantin els camins».
Si jo sabés, benastruga,
trobar un camí pelegrí!
Sal de llàgrima aturada
no em couria als ulls. I visc
perquè la nit no és eterna.
Desperta dintre la nit
mirava. I el nus d'angoixa
ja era una mort en mi;
els ulls van a la finestra,
quan en un punt ha lluit
la llum de la matinada.

WAKING AT DEAD OF NIGHT

Waking at dead of night,
I open my eyes. Were it not for the pain…
the room has come to life within its walls,
I feel the touch of darkness on my face,
hear woodworm burrowing into the bed,
and smell sea air from the cove –
a breath of it, come to join me…
if all this anguish did not rack me so,
I could spread and stretch out.
But in the blackness I can see
all I've longed for, lost –
through my own fault…
I could beat my breast for shame.
Who, now, is going to call me
the 'strong woman' I never claimed to be?
What unknown sea is destiny
arranging for me to cross?
I can see a far-off procession –
…oleanders, tamarinds…
and hands, beckoning to me,
Have no fear of the road, come travel with us.
Oh, what a blessing it would be
to know my pilgrim way!
My eyes would not be salt
with held-back tears. I only live
because the dark does not go on for ever.
Waking at dead of night,
eyes wide open, the knot of pain
withering, like a corpse, inside me,
I let my gaze drift to the window
and there's a speck, a gleam
of dawning light.

COMANDA A UN ARGENTER

Per a Ramon Sunyer, argenter

Ai rosa, la meva rosa,
amb el pinyol cora lí!
Passeu les roses discretes,
avui no sóc com ahir.
Que jo vull aquella rosa
que no és al meu jardí:
vull la rosa cisellada
amb el pinyol cora lí
flairós encara de platja
i de besar submarí.
Rosa pomposa de plata
tota estriada d'or fi!
Única que serves
caliu de mà i de burí
i una mica la mirada
que creava el teu destí!

Per la teva humana força
si vinguessis cap a mi,
oh rosa, la meva rosa,
amb el pinyol coralí!

THE COMMISSION

for R. Sunyer, silversmith

Oh rose, my own dear rose,
with a heart of coral!
I've had enough of sober roses –
I'm different these days.
Now I'm looking for the kind
that won't grow in my garden –
I want that finely-crafted rose
with its heart of coral,
fresh with the scent of the sea's edge
and an underwater kiss.
Sumptuous rose of silver
with delicate streaks of gold!
Singular rose, still warm
from hand and burin's touch,
and still with something of the gaze
that forged your destiny!

Oh, that your own human power
could bring you to me –
rose, my own sweet rose,
with your heart of coral!

EL POEMA FELIÇ

Deliberadament
tanquem la porta; –
a fora, el sol i el vent,
els camps i l'horta;
a dins, molt sola i molt endins,
la Meravella;
ardent, la soledad
es lliga amb ella.
Per qué?
A l'ombra del no-re
uns mots suscita,
i acuden com ocells
tots a la cita
els mots,
alegres o capcots
– oh quina tria! –
La prova cal del foc
i l'agonia.
Després,
es tanca al seu recès,
misteriosa,
i neix – quin temps més llarg! –
com d'una fosa
d'encís,
el poema feliç.
«Mare que bleixa,
Meravella – direm –
vida mateixa
ets tu»;
però no ho sap ningú.

Deliberadament
tanquem la porta;
a fora, el sol i el vent,
els camps i l'horta.

THE POEM

With mind
made up, let's close the door;
outside, the sun, the wind,
the fields,the kitchen garden.
In here,
all alone and far within,
the Miracle,
in league with a searing,
passionate solitude.
Why? –
In the depths of shadowy Nothing
their union gives rise
to words – which turn up like birds
flocking together,
words
downcast or blithe – and
oh, how they must be
sifted! a trial of fire,
an agony.
Next,
the Miracle closes her own door
in mysterious retreat, and then
(what an age it takes!)
in a kind of magical smelting,
the poem
is born.
"O Miracle, still-panting
Mother," we'll exclaim –
"You are Life
itself!"
But no one, no one knows…

With mind
made up, let's close the door;
outside, the sun, the wind,
the fields, the kitchen garden.

FERMANÇA

Passa l'amor com una aigua,
   jo el sé meu del pont estant,
si n'aixeca la mirada,
   jo l'anava interrogant:

«No portessis tanta pressa,
   bé em diries mon pecat.
¿Per què, el vidre que estimava,
   ara el veig esmiscolat?

¿Fou el vent que el decantava
   o fou el meu braç, rabent?
Digues-me també l'angoixa
   que em nua l'enteniment.

Tu que pots, ¿per què no em dones…?
   Però callo, parles tu.»
«Mai no esperis que jo et salvi
   pensament o cristall nu.

Tu mateixa passa l'aigua,
   no t'aturis dalt del pont;
porta el cantiret enlaire,
   vigila'l fins a la font.

I si vénen fumaroles
   que t'entelin els sentits,
fes un vot de fe lliurada
   i esvaeix-les amb els dits.

Jo ara et dono la paraula
   d'ésser teu fins a la fi,
mentre corro com una aigua
   que segueix el seu camí.»

RESOLVE

Running like water in a brook
Love's mine, I'm sure, as long as I look
down from the bridge. But as soon as Love
looks up, I'm full of questions:

"If only you were in less haste,
you'd make it clear how I've transgressed:
what has shattered the clear glass,
the crystal I cherished?

Was it the wind that toppled it,
or my own arm, too hasty?
Tell me why such torment twists
and knots my wits –

you can tell, so why, oh why,
won't you? – Answer, I'll be quiet."
"You hope I'll salvage your lost thought,
your crystal glass? – Never, not I.

Wade the stream yourself, don't dally
up on the bridge, but raise
your water-jar, and hold it steady
till you reach the source.

If vapours rise, and you are lost
in the mists, misled,
then with an act of perfect trust
brush them aside.

I now give you my solemn word –
to the very end, I will be yours –
while, running like water in a brook,
I follow my own course."

ORIOL

Somni que el moment exalta!
Ahir
volia fuir de mi.
Somni d'una tarda blanca!
Avui
com podria dir «no vui»,
quan és certa ja l'espera?
Son cor –
petit cor secret, tan fort
que, no nat, ja no li esqueia –
em diu:
«Assossega el cor i riu;
passa el pont, que a l'altre riba
seré
i d'ánima em vestiré.
Tu diràs, esbalaïda:
Ben nat:
pel polit i l'acabat,
Déu et valgui, criatura».
Ahir, avui, son cor
em diu: «Seré ben nat».
I en acabat,
la Joia.

ORIOL

Dream, suddenly made glorious!
Yesterday
I couldn't face myself.
Reverie of an empty afternoon!
Today
how can I say
'No,' – now I'm really expecting him?
His heart –
his tiny, secret heart, so strong,
even before he's born, it doesn't waver –
whispers to me:
Steady yourself, be of good cheer;
cross the bridge to the other side –
there I shall be,
and I shall put on life.
You'll be amazed – you'll say,
'Welcome, newborn:
so perfect, so complete –
God bless you, little one.'
Yesterday, today, his heart
keeps telling me, *I'll be born,*
all shall be well – and then
the Jewel, then the Joy.

De la nit i el mar

Nit,
porta secreta fora el pit,
no et tanca pany ni corda;
silenci que recorda,
nit,
només voltada d'infinit.

Vés,
si tu t'avances, jo després
puc avarar la barca
– un àngel lleu la marca;
fes
que jo navegui sempre més.

Nit,
amb el teu cel de fit a fit
i la humitat amarga!
Amb quina joia llarga,
pit,
alenaràs el mot oblit!

Rar,
dintre la nit, la vasta mar
poder solcar, lliberta;
viure a ple cor, alerta,
mar
i nit, la sal del vostre empar!

Night and the Sea

Night,
secret door out of the heart
no chain or bolt can lock;
silence of remembrance,
boundless
night.

If you lead on,
look
how I launch my boat,
its mark, a minor angel;
O make me
sail on, ever further out.

Night
with your eyeball-to-eyeball sky,
your bitter mist!
In what slow rapture,
heart,
you'll breathe the long-forgotten word!

How strange,
in the dark night,
to ply the vast ocean, free,
full-hearted, open-eyed,
alive in your salt shelter,
Night and Sea.

ARA

Ara que ja de tanta cosa torno…
No em pregunteu, que no sabria dir-vos
per quina brida m'he sentit lligada.
El cor encara vol tornar a gronxar-se
desbocat a les barques de la fira;
i dic que sí, que en mi tot clama d'esma
cap aquella petita esbojarrada.
… I ja no sóc sinó una dona absorta,
amb la veu i amb el riure que s'aturen.

NOW

Now I must turn aside from oh, so much…
don't ask, I can't explain
this tugging of a rein that keeps me tethered –
and still, my heart is longing to soar again,
swoop up and over on a fairground swing –
and I say, YES: my whole instinctive being
cries out towards that wild, untamed girl!
…And now I'm just a daydreamer, a woman
with a voice that fades, a laugh cut short.

PER NO CAURE

Per no caure mai més
– i és avui que jo queia;
la caiguda pensable
ja vindrà certament –
em cal fer, més que passos,
intents.

Un designi de vol
per damunt de la terra,
un esquinç de rialla
en els llavis, i el cos
planejant com per l'aire
mai clos.

Per no caure mai més
poso el cor en reserva
– pobre cor massa tendre
dins un fang massa vell! –
en campana de vidre
tot ell.

DON'T FALL

Never to fall again –
and I stumbled only today;
only think of a fall
and a fall will come –
rather than taking steps, I need
aims.

A blueprint, for flying high
above the earth:
the twist of a smile
on my lips, and my body
gliding as if through air, free
as a bird.

Never to fall again,
my heart must be held back –
poor heart, too tender
in muddy clay, too old by far!
And all kept under a bell-
jar.

ABRES

Sóc amb vosaltres, arbres folls en la nit,
sento que el vent us té desperta i us força.
Jo també vetllo, perquè em puny el delit
d'interrogar en aquest concert ferotge.
Trona i llampega. Mare meva del cel,
quina cortina d'aigua viva tan fosca!
El vers començ, fa un caminar rebel,
torça i retorça, que vol eixir al defora.
Els arbres baten, i jo estic a aixopluc.
Van les preguntes cap al dia amb les hores.
Deixo fer el vers, ja no sé què més puc
sinó escoltar que el temperi redobla.
Demà, renta'ls amb les fulles lluents
– passat el vers per un sedàs d'aurora –
podrem reprendre els co loquis ardents,
arbres gentils d'escabellades tofes.

TREES

I'm with you, trees, mad and wild in the night,
I hear how the wind wakes you, forces itself on you.
I'm wide awake too, spurred by the sheer delight
of questioning, while this fierce concert rages.
Thunder and lightning… O Mother in Heaven,
what pitch-dark curtains of living water!
My poem sets out on a rebellious trek,
twisting and turning, and longing to get out;
the trees thrash, and I'm here under cover.
Questions run on toward day as each hour passes –
I leave my poem, it seems all I can do
is listen as the storm redoubles its force…
Tomorrow, washed clean, our leaves all shining –
my scribbled lines sieved by the morning light –
we shall resume our burning colloquies,
O graceful trees, with your dishevelled crowns.

L'ESPERANÇA ENCARA DANSA

L'esperança encara dansa
al voltant del meu amor,
gira, tomba, quan s'atansa,
no hi val ombra, ni recança.
Fina daga, doloret,
fes-te enllà i el coll avança:
no t'en riguis, que l'amor
posa flors a la balança.
Cabell blanc sigui en la dansa
aliret i cant d'ocell.
Galta pa lida mostrant-se –
fes-la roja tu, esperança.
I per sempre dansa, dansa.

HOPE KEEPS DANCING

Hope keeps dancing – never stopping –
dancing round and round my love,
wheeling, diving, spinning, hopping,
till shadows pale and shrink to nothing.
Pangs of grief, stiletto-fine,
go on, go and do your worst:
no holding back – remember, love
brings flowers to even out the balance.
This dance lets old age and white hair
hee-haw like donkeys, chirrup like birds.
The cheek that blanches pale and droops,
Hope, make her blush again– and Hope
keep dancing – dance and never stop.

AL BON PAPA JOAN XXIII

Volíeu «Pau a la terra»
– Déu n'hi do!
I l'Esposa desguarníeu
d'enfarfecs.
Vestit nou calia dar-li
provident
i fer-la més «Mare i Mestra»
per a tots.

Obeixen les paraules
a la veu,
són com una torrentada
quan us cal,
o silenci en vós s'enginya
com un fre.
L'amor de Déu i dels homes
vau tenir.

To the Good Pope, John XXIII

You wanted *Peace on Earth* –
God grant it!
And you stripped away the paraphernalia
burdening Christ's Bride:
time to give her something new
to wear, simpler and more measured,
so she could be more truly *Queen and Mother*
to us all.

Your words came in obedience
to your voice –
when needed, they
ran streaming out,
or a silence welled in you,
applied its brake.
So full of love you were – for God
and for the people.

Espera, encara

La Mort m'ha fet com un eixut,
per sempre.
Ja no hi ha ocells, no hi ha cap flor
que es gronxi:
d'aquest ermot van aflorant
les pedres.
I sento encara aquella veu
que em guia!,
Tinc les paraules que escrigué
i em resten!,
però no trobo aquella mà
segura,
forta i benigne, purament
oferta.
Arravatada, no puc més,
em giro…
Àngels de Déu puc albirar
que em miren,
pleguen les ales i amb els ulls
em diuen:
«Encara et manca més virtut,
espera.»

Still Hope (Wait Still)

Death has wrung me dry
for good.
No birds now, not a single flower
stirring:
in this desert nothing blooms
but stones.
And even now, that voice –
my guide!
I have the very words he wrote,
still with me!
But not his hand,
safe, sound,
held out so simply.
In a storm of rage
I halt. No more – I can't.
I start to turn…
Dimly I can make out
God's angels, staring.
They fold down their wings and speak
with eyes alone:
Not yet – be stronger still.
Wait. Hope.

L'ESPERANÇA, ENCARA

En la meva donzellesa
ja et portava dins el pit,
Esperança, Confiança,
moviment de l'esperit!
«Sempre invoca l'esperança –
diu un crític – i de què?»
Mai no m'he sentit ben sola
que Esperança vol dir Fe.
I la casa se'm fa ampla
quan aquest vent s'hi expandeix,
alades paraules sento,
veig l'arbre que refloreix.
En la meva viduesa
no vull ombres al meu dol.
He estat i sóc encara
dona que viu a ple sol.
La nit es lliga amb el dia
i et sé tan sovint amb mi!
Que volo, somnio i sento
com si encara fos ahir.
Si el meu Carles m'enamora –
oh Esperança! –
tu encara dius que sí.

Unfailing Hope

Even as a young girl
I held you in my heart,
Hope, Trust,
Spirit's fluency!
A critic says, "She always calls
on Hope – in hope of what?"
I have never felt alone
because, for me, Hope means
Faith. My house is roomier
when that breeze stirs within;
I hear words on the wing,
my tree blossoms again.
In widowhood, I'll mourn
but not be gloomy.
I am, as I have always been,
a woman living out in the sun.
Now Night draws close to Day,
and you're so often with me
that I can fly, and dream, and feel
as if it were still yesterday.
If my Carles keeps me in love –
oh, Hope! –
you will say, *Yes*.